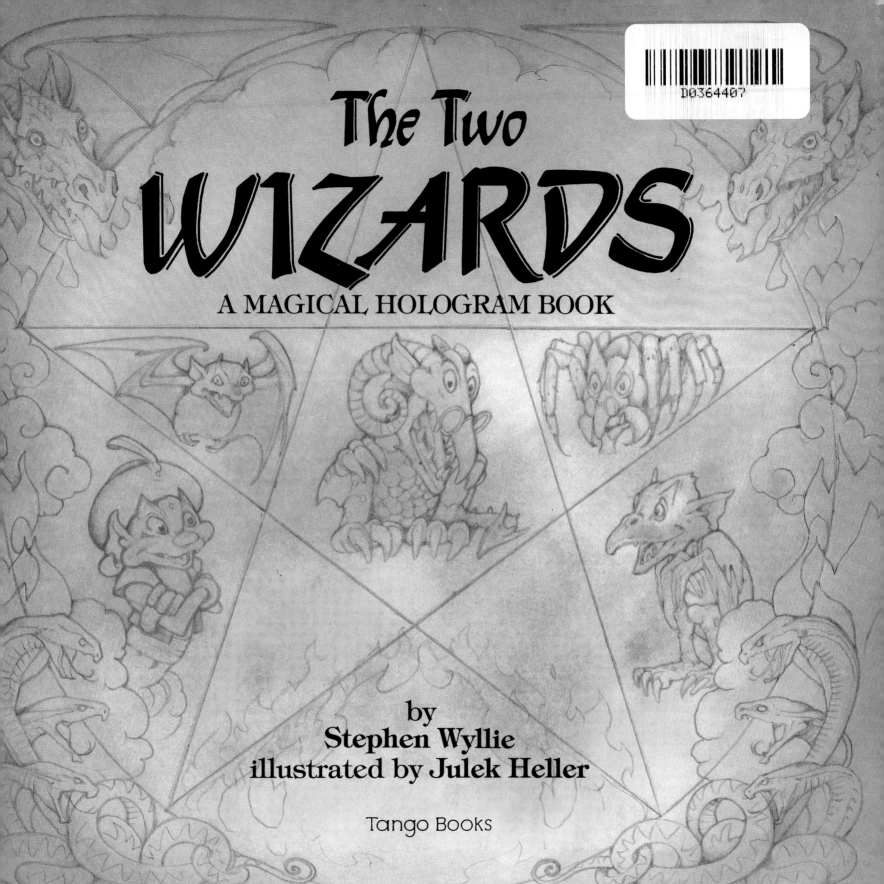

The Two WIZARDS

A MAGICAL HOLOGRAM BOOK

by
Stephen Wyllie
illustrated by **Julek Heller**

Tango Books

For many years, Karamazool had been a happy wizard. He was always ready, for a small fee, to cure warts, find lost jewellery and cast all sorts of spells for the people who lived in his town.

But that was until wizard Andropos bought the house next door and everyone took their problems to him to find out if he was any better.

"What can I do?" he asked himself. "If this goes on much longer, I'll starve."

He took a black velvet cloth and rubbed his crystal ball. "Oh genie of the crystal ball," he intoned, "how can I stop Andropos from stealing all my customers?"

The genie appeared. "I could turn him into a spooky bat for three days," he suggested.

"Excellent idea," said Karamazool. "Go ahead."

There was a brilliant flash and
Karamazool ran outside to peer
through Andropos's window. Sure
enough, an enormous ghostly bat
was sitting on top of the bookshelf,
flapping its wings.

When no one answered Andropos's door, the townsfolk thought he had gone away, and they went back to seeing Karamazool. But after three days there was another brilliant flash and Andropos turned back into a wizard: a wizard bent on revenge.

He took his magic mirror from a drawer and set it on his desk. "Oh goblin of the mirror," he chanted, "show me how to get even with Karamazool."
The goblin appeared. "A brief spell as a hairy spider might teach him a lesson," he replied.
"Wonderful!" said Andropos. "Let's go for it."

The goblin snapped his fingers and there was a loud bang. Andropos rushed outside to look through Karamazool's letterbox. The eight eyes of an enormous hairy spider were looking straight back at him.

"Oh goody," said Andropos, rubbing his hands together. People came back to see him again, convinced that Karamazool had closed down.

A few days later, the spell wore off and, in a puff of smoke, the spider disappeared and a hopping mad Karamazool returned. The confused people of the town began to visit both Karamazool and Andropos – but the two wizards were determined to get the better of each other.

Andropos knew that Karamazool would
want to get even, so he drilled a small spy-hole
in the wall which divided their two
laboratories in the hope of cancelling any
spell that Karamazool might try to cast.

One day, when Andropos's eye was glued to the peep-hole, he saw Karamazool rubbing his crystal ball. He quickly reached for his magic mirror.

"Oh genie of the crystal ball," said Karamazool.

"Oh goblin of the magic mirror," said Andropos. "Banish Andropos." "Banish Karamazool," they said together – "to Inner Earth."

"My pleasure," said the genie, and the goblin snapped his fingers.

There was an enormous bang and Karamazool and Andropos tumbled through space amid rolls of thunder and flashes of lightning. They landed, with a bump, side by side in Inner Earth.